D1541809

STEAM JOBS IN
SPACE
EXPLORATION

Ray Reyes

Rourke
Educational Media

rourkeeducationalmedia.com

Before Reading:

Building Academic Vocabulary and Background Knowledge

Before reading a book, it is important to tap into what your child or students already know about the topic. This will help them develop their vocabulary, increase their reading comprehension, and make connections across the curriculum.

1. *Look at the cover of the book. What will this book be about?*
2. *What do you already know about the topic?*
3. *Let's study the Table of Contents. What will you learn about in the book's chapters?*
4. *What would you like to learn about this topic? Do you think you might learn about it from this book? Why or why not?*
5. *Use a reading journal to write about your knowledge of this topic. Record what you already know about the topic and what you hope to learn about the topic.*
6. *Read the book.*
7. *In your reading journal, record what you learned about the topic and your response to the book.*
8. *After reading the book complete the activities below.*

Content Area Vocabulary
Read the list. What do these words mean?

aerospace
avionics
composite
extrasolar
extraterrestrial
pressurized
prototype
radiation
subatomic
vacuum

After Reading:

Comprehension and Extension Activity

After reading the book, work on the following questions with your child or students in order to check their level of reading comprehension and content mastery.

1. *What jobs do astronauts perform in space? (Summarize)*
2. *Why do astronomers study galaxies and stars? (Infer)*
3. *How does visible light break down into a spectrum? (Asking Questions)*
4. *Would you rather choose to be an astronaut or astronomer? Why or why not? (Text to Self Connection)*
5. *What is the role of a payload specialist? (Asking Questions)*

Extension Activity

Make your own model of the solar system! Take a trip to your local museum to view a solar system model research our solar system online. Then have an adult help you to gather materials to make your own mode of the solar system, featuring all eight planets and maybe their moons. Follow the instructions at http://blog hobbycraft.co.uk/how-to-make-a-model-solar-system/ for ideas!

Table of Contents

What is STEAM?

Astronauts on space stations conduct scientific experiments in zero gravity. On Earth, engineers design communication, software, and energy systems for spacesuits. Astronomers peer through telescopes to understand the origin of the universe. They use computers to download data from robotic spacecraft at the edge of the solar system.

What do these people have in common? They work in the exciting field of space exploration. Their jobs require a STEAM education, which is vital if you want to work in outer space, learn about stars and galaxies, or explore the solar system.

What does STEAM stand for?

Science
Technology
Engineering
Art
Math

Some of the most exciting careers are in STEAM fields. A strong STEAM education can help you develop theories, design new things, or improve existing technology. Whether they're in orbit or on Earth, space explorers draw upon their STEAM education to help grow our knowledge about the universe.

Engineers inspect components of the James Webb Space Telescope, which is the successor to the Hubble Space Telescope.

Astronauts spend years training on Earth to develop skills to work in orbit or on the International Space Station.

The Final Frontier

For thousands of years, human beings looked up and wondered what was beyond the clouds. We found out in the 20th century, when the first astronauts launched into space. Astronauts confirmed theories that space was a **vacuum**. They discovered that stars shine clearer beyond Earth's atmosphere. This new knowledge paved the way for an entire fleet of space-based telescopes.

STEAM Fast Fact:

The first human in space was Russian cosmonaut Yuri Gagarin. He made a 108-minute orbital flight around Earth in the *Vostok 1* spacecraft on April 12, 1961. Thirty-four years later, Valery Polyakov, another Russian cosmonaut, set a record for spending 438 consecutive days in space. Can you imagine living in outer space for more than a year?

Yuri Gagarin
1934 – 1968

Real STEAM Job:
Astronaut

Astronauts do their jobs in space, but they spend a lot of time on the ground training and studying. The National Aeronautics and Space Administration, or NASA, screens thousands of aspiring astronauts every year. NASA even looks for candidates with degrees in archaeology or geography! The candidates undergo physical and psychological tests to ensure they can work and survive in outer space.

While some astronauts like Thomas Pesquet are pilots or engineers, some are scientists who conduct experiments in space.

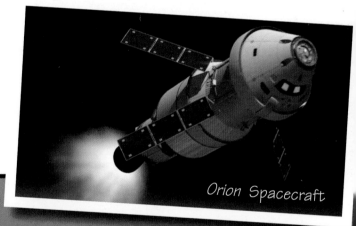

Orion Spacecraft

STEAM Fast Fact:

NASA has only selected 339 candidates out of thousands of applicants to become astronauts since the program was founded in 1959. Some of them became the first Americans to orbit Earth and the first astronauts to land on the moon. NASA's current astronaut candidates are training to go farther. The space agency plans to send humans to Mars in the 2030s, and its engineers are developing the *Orion* spacecraft to send them there. One day maybe you can live and work on the Red Planet!

STEAM Spotlight

Astronauts in the United States train at the Johnson Space Center (JSC) in Houston, Texas, which was built in 1963. The JSC is the home of the famous Apollo program, which sent astronauts to the moon. It's also hosted the space shuttle program, which lasted for 30 years and was retired in 2011. The space center houses the Mission Control Center, which communicates with astronauts in space. But its coolest feature? The Neutral Buoyancy Laboratory, a large pool that is 202 feet (61.57 meters) long, 102 feet (31 meters) wide, 40 feet (12 meters) deep, and holds 6.2 million gallons (23,469,553 liters) of water. The pool simulates a zero-gravity environment like outer space.

NASA trains astronauts and oversees missions at the Johnson Space Center in Texas.

An astronaut trains in the Johnson Space Center's pool.

Some astronauts are experienced pilots with military backgrounds. Others are engineers, who make sure power systems are always up and running. Another group of space explorers are called payload specialists. They have degrees in medicine, biology, physics, and other fields.

Real STEAM Job: *Payload Specialist*

Payload specialists are selected outside of NASA's regular astronaut candidate program. According to NASA, payload specialists have studied air pollution from orbit, observed weather patterns on Earth, mapped the oceans, and researched how our bodies function in zero gravity. Some payload specialists have even brought insects to outer space to see how they behave!

Payload specialist Roberta Bondar, left, observes an experiment in a space shuttle's microgravity lab.

SUITED FOR SPACE

Many scientists and engineers work in laboratories on Earth designing equipment and vehicles for space travel.

Mechanical engineers built the robot explorers that roam Mars looking for evidence of water or **extraterrestrial** life. Engineers continue to improve the designs of spacesuits, rocket systems, and spacecraft.

Mars *Curiosity* rover

Real STEAM Job: *Spacesuit Engineer*

Astronauts wear bulky spacesuits ideal for going outside space shuttles or space stations. The suits provide oxygen and a **pressurized** atmosphere like Earth's to protect them from **radiation** and the vacuum of space. They were built specifically for missions in low Earth orbit.

Now that NASA and other space agencies are planning trips to other planets, more flexible and mobile spacesuits are needed to explore those environments.

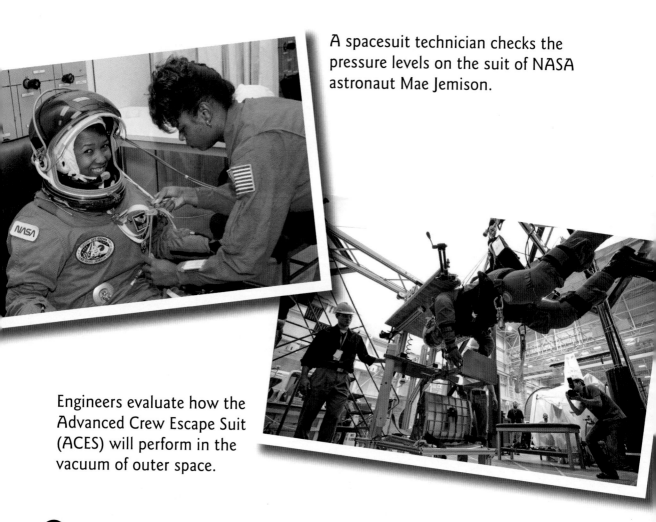

A spacesuit technician checks the pressure levels on the suit of NASA astronaut Mae Jemison.

Engineers evaluate how the Advanced Crew Escape Suit (ACES) will perform in the vacuum of outer space.

STEAM in Action!

Have you ever wondered what it feels like to wear an astronaut's spacesuit? All you need are two long balloons and three heavy duty rubber bands.

Take the first balloon and inflate it. The balloon is like the pressure bladder in a spacesuit's arm. How stiff is the balloon? Is it easy to bend? Now take the second balloon and inflate it too. Place the three rubber bands along its length, evenly spaced, until those segments tied by the rubber bands pinch and puff out. Try bending the balloon with the rubber bands. Is it easier to bend than the first? How do the two balloons feel compared to a mattress, an inner tube, or a beach ball?

Engineers discovered that to help astronauts bend their arms and legs in space, those parts of a pressurized spacesuit need segments for better flexibility. So the balloon with the rubber bands is similar to the arms and legs found on a real spacesuit!

Engineers rely on their knowledge of physics, chemistry, or electrical engineering to build durable spacesuits that can last for hundreds of days in harsh conditions. Improved power systems, computer software, and life support systems are in development for these **prototype** suits.

STEAM Spotlight

Spacesuits may look like giant marshmallows, but every inch of the equipment was developed to ensure maximum protection in space. In orbit around Earth, it can get as cold as minus 250 degrees Fahrenheit (minus 121 degrees Celsius). When astronauts find themselves on the sunny side of the planet, it can get as hot as 275 degrees Fahrenheit (135 degrees Celsius) in direct sunlight.

Spacesuit materials include stainless steel, nylon, spandex, and Mylar. Some parts are sewn or cemented together. Others are joined by metal components.

It takes about 45 minutes to put on a spacesuit. This is called "donning" the suit. Astronauts must also put on special undergarments that help keep them cool. Taking off a spacesuit is known as "doffing."

And yes, spacesuits are extremely bulky. On Earth, they can weigh as much as 280 pounds (127 kilograms). Of course, in space, they weigh nothing. And the reason why they're all white and look like marshmallows? White reflects heat better than any other color, just like on Earth.

We Are Go For Launch

Astronauts can't do their jobs unless they have a way to leave Earth. That task belongs to **aerospace** engineers. They design the spacecraft that carry people to outer space. Aerospace engineers are experts in specific fields, such as materials science, which focuses on building stronger and lighter equipment.

Aerospace engineers built the rockets that took astronauts to the moon. They built the space shuttles that placed satellites in orbit. And they built space stations where astronauts live and work in zero gravity.

STEAM Fast Fact:

The laws of physics that govern rocketry were conceived by Sir Isaac Newton in 1687. The British astronomer, mathematician, and physicist formulated what's now known as Newton's Three Laws of Motion.

Law 1: An object at rest will remain at rest and an object in motion will remain in motion unless acted upon by an unbalanced force.

Law 2: Force equals mass times acceleration (or in equation form, $f=ma$).

Law 3: For every action there is an equal and opposite reaction.

Spacecraft and satellites are assembled in clean rooms, which block out dust and moisture.

STEAM Spotlight

Although astronauts train at the Johnson Space Center in Texas, their trip to space begins at the Kennedy Space Center (KSC) in Cape Canaveral, Florida. The KSC is the only facility in the U.S. where NASA—and now, private companies such as SpaceX—launch rockets and other spacecraft.

Missions to the moon, the Skylab space laboratory, and all the space shuttles were launched from the KSC. Today, unmanned rockets launch from the space center to deliver supplies to the International Space Station (ISS).

The KSC's most unique feature is the vehicle assembly building (VAB), where moon rockets and the space shuttles were built. This building is so large at more than 129 million cubic feet (3,652,873 cubic meters) that it is known as the tallest single-story building in the world. Standing 526 feet (160.325 meters) tall, the VAB is the tallest building in the U.S. outside of an urban area. It was the tallest building in Florida until a taller luxury hotel was built in Miami in 1974.

You can even see the VAB for yourself! The KSC, just like the JSC in Texas, is a popular tourist attraction. Thousands of visitors visit these space centers every year to learn more about the history and future of space travel.

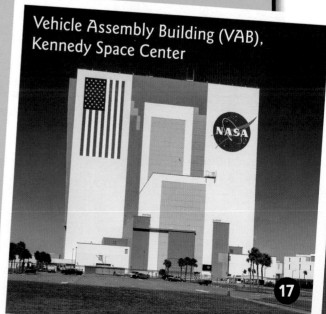

Vehicle Assembly Building (VAB), Kennedy Space Center

Real STEAM Job: *Avionics Engineer*

Avionics engineers design, build, and test the parts that allow explorers to maneuver above Earth or travel to other worlds.

Avionics systems include computers for communication. These let astronauts talk to mission control centers on the ground. Avionics engineers also build weather radar and collision-detection systems, increasing safety for all flights.

Avionics engineers design and build communication and flight systems, such as the ones used in Cape Canaveral's Launch Control Center.

STEAM in Action!

Getting a small model rocket off the ground or a giant metal NASA rocket into space involves the same principles. Aerospace engineers are experts in the laws of gravity and motion. They know exactly how much fuel is needed to launch all kinds of rockets.

You can build a simple rocket yourself and see how the basic principles of air pressure and force affect rocket design. All you need is an empty plastic bottle, cardboard, a cork, a tire pump with a needle adapter, some water, and protective goggles to cover your eyes. Make sure an adult is around, because this rocket will really take off!

Use the cardboard to craft four fins and a cone. Tape the cone to the bottom of the bottle. Tape the fins around the other end of the bottle. Push the tire pump needle all the way into the cork. Fill the bottle rocket with one quarter full of water and close the bottle using the cork with the needle through it.

Now stand back—and tell anyone watching to stand back—and start pumping until the rocket takes off. How high did the rocket fly? How many times did you have to use the tire pump until the rocket took off?

Real STEAM Job: *Materials Engineer*

Materials engineers build rocket parts made from **composite** materials. Composites use two or more materials to make something stronger. Engineers use composites of carbon and silicon for tiles that protect spacecraft from the heat and friction caused by reentering the Earth's atmosphere.

An animation to the right of the SpaceX *Dragon* V2 spacecraft shows how the vessel would withstand re-entry into the Earth's atmosphere.

Materials engineers designed advanced foam for NASA space shuttles, which insulated the craft from the cold and heat of outer space.

STEAM Spotlight

NASA scientists and engineers are always coming up with ways to make stronger and lighter materials for space travel. In one test, an 8.4 foot (2.56 meter) barrel made of composite materials was crushed with 900,000 pounds (4,082 kilograms) of force to see how long it would last under so much pressure.

The goal? To perfect the design of rockets made of composite materials, so heavier payloads of food, water, fuel, and other supplies can be sent into space. The more supplies rockets can carry, the likelier a manned trip to Mars becomes a reality, according to NASA.

Strange New Worlds

You don't have to travel to outer space to explore the wonders of the universe. In fact, the distances between planets, stars, and solar systems are so vast that it is impractical to send people to those far-flung worlds.

Instead, astronomers, physicists, and cosmologists work in laboratories and observatories to study other planets and galaxies. Some of these scientists work with space agencies to build robotic spacecraft or space telescopes to study **extrasolar** planets, black holes, and other wonders.

STEAM Fast Fact:

Galileo was the first astronomer to build his own telescope and point it at the sky in 1609. With this tool, Galileo could view the mountains and craters on the moon. He could also study Jupiter and its four largest moons. Galileo's observations helped him prove that the sun was the center of the solar system, not the Earth.

Galileo
1564 – 1642

STEAM Spotlight

Astronomers don't use miles or kilometers to describe the distance of objects in space, because the universe is so big. Instead they use light years, which measures the distance that light travels in a year.

Light travels 186,000 miles (299,338 kilometers) per second. There are 60 seconds in a minute and 60 minutes in an hour. There are 24 hours in a day and 365 days in a year. When you multiply all of that together, you get 31,500,000 seconds in one year. Now multiply that by 186,000 miles (299,338 kilometers) per second and you'll see that light travels about 6 trillion miles (9,656,064,000,000 kilomters) in one year!

The closest star to Earth is called Alpha Centauri, which is 4.3 light years away. How far away in miles is this star?

The center of our own galaxy, the Milky Way, is about 25,000 light years away. Can you imagine how long it would take to drive a car to the center of our galaxy?

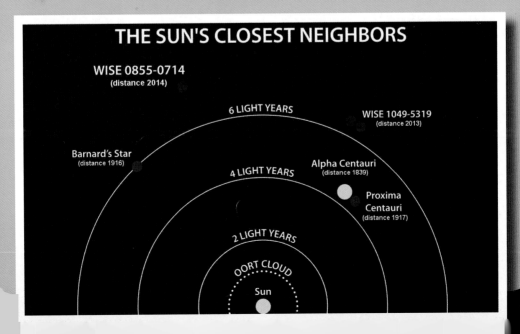

THE SUN'S CLOSEST NEIGHBORS

Real STEAM Job: *Observational Astronomer*

Astronomers who use different kinds of telescopes to view objects in the universe are known as observational astronomers. These astronomers work at observatories with optical or radio telescopes to directly observe stars and galaxies. Observational astronomers have discovered asteroids, comets, and even dwarf planets like Pluto!

Mauna Kea observatories, Hawaii

STEAM in Action!

Do you want to know what astronomers see when they look up into the night sky? All you need is a free star map app for tablets, or an interactive map you can search for online.

The constellations you can see depend on the time of year. That's because the Earth revolves around the sun while constellations appear fixed in the sky.

One of the most famous constellations is Ursa Major, or the Big Dipper. Use your star map to find this constellation, which is visible most times of the year. What does it look like to you? Can you tell why it's called the Big Dipper?

Another famous constellation is Orion the Hunter, which is visible in the winter sky. Again, use your star map to find this group of stars. What do you see? Is Orion bigger or smaller than you expected it to be?

What other constellations, stars, or planets can you find with your star map?

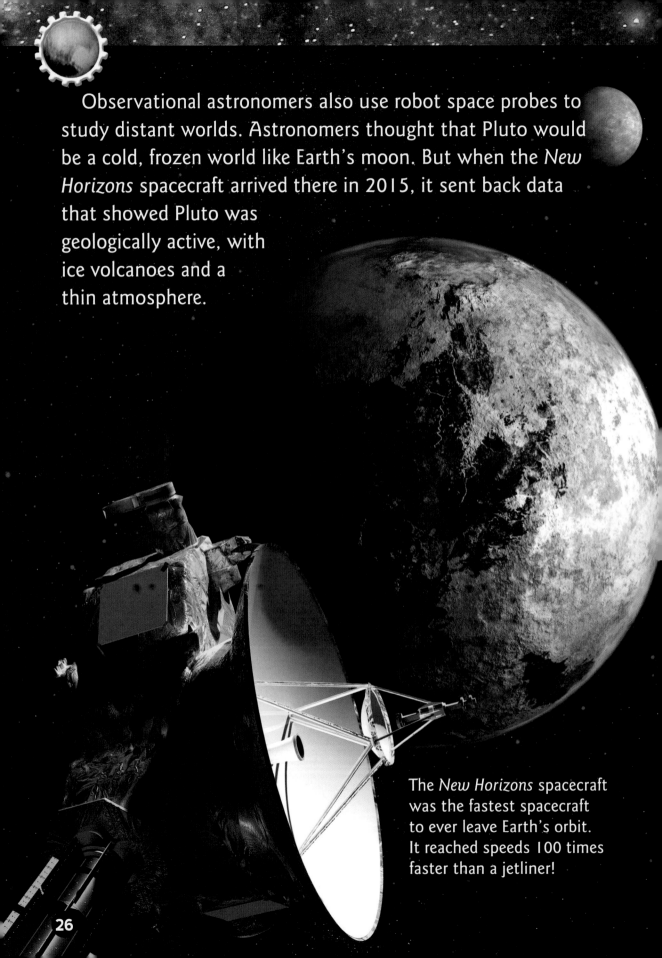

Observational astronomers also use robot space probes to study distant worlds. Astronomers thought that Pluto would be a cold, frozen world like Earth's moon. But when the *New Horizons* spacecraft arrived there in 2015, it sent back data that showed Pluto was geologically active, with ice volcanoes and a thin atmosphere.

The *New Horizons* spacecraft was the fastest spacecraft to ever leave Earth's orbit. It reached speeds 100 times faster than a jetliner!

Real STEAM Job: *Spacecraft Engineer*

Spacecraft engineers work on the power, propulsion, and computer systems of probes to ensure they reach their destination and collect data efficiently.

Spacecraft engineers built robots that scanned the surface of Venus, dove into the thick clouds of Jupiter, and flew into the icy dust tails of comets. And their work is never done! NASA plans future missions to the asteroid belt and the moons of Saturn.

STEAM Fast Fact:

NASA has invited the public to download and process images from the Juno space probe's mission to Jupiter. Go to https://www.missionjuno.swri. edu/junocam/processing/ and you can edit the images like actual NASA imaging specialists then share them with the space agency!

STEAM Fast Fact:

Voyager 1 and 2, twin probes launched in the late 1970s, are now the most distant manmade objects in space. The tiny space probes first visited the outer planets in our solar system. They are now headed for interstellar space, the region of space outside our system, and between the nearest stars.

Voyager 1 is about 11.5 billion miles (18,507,456,000 kilometers) away from Earth while Voyager 2 is about 9.5 billion miles (15,288,768,000 kilometers).

STEAM Spotlight

The Hubble Space Telescope is a breakthrough in observational astronomy. It is expanding our knowledge of the universe. Named after astronomer Edwin Hubble, the world's most famous telescope was launched in low Earth orbit in 1990.

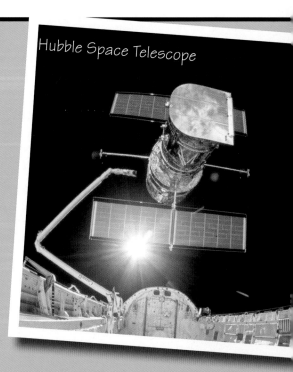

Hubble Space Telescope

One of the Hubble Space Telescope's most startling discoveries, called the Hubble Deep View, was that even if a patch of night sky looks completely empty, it is filled with clusters of stars—and the oldest galaxies ever seen by astronomers.

Only scientists have access to a telescope as powerful as Hubble, but you can observe your own "deep view" using simple binoculars.

Look at one section of the night sky with just your eyes. How many stars can you count? Next, point the binoculars at the same section of sky. What's different?

You can increase the deep view with a basic telescope. So, if you have one, use it. And remember to write down your observations!

The Hubble launched with a defect in its mirrors, which were made to take high-resolution photographs. Instead, the photos were blurry. NASA astronauts fixed the mirror in a 1993 mission.

Since then, the Hubble made startling discoveries. The telescope confirmed that the universe is 13.7 billion years old. The Hubble proved theories that black holes, a region in space with such intense gravity that not even light can escape it, not only exist, but that they are common throughout the universe.

The Hubble is still in operation today. Observational astronomers continue to use the space telescope to help them prove theories and view distant galaxies.

Searching for E.T.'s

One branch of astronomy focuses on the search for habitable planets outside of our solar system and the evidence of intelligent life beyond Earth. One of the most famous projects, the Search for Extraterrestrial Life, or SETI, uses telescopes to scan for radio or electromagnetic signals from alien civilizations.

Other astronomers focus on data and photographs obtained by robot spacecraft sent to other worlds to see if microscopic lifeforms like bacteria can exist on moons around other planets.

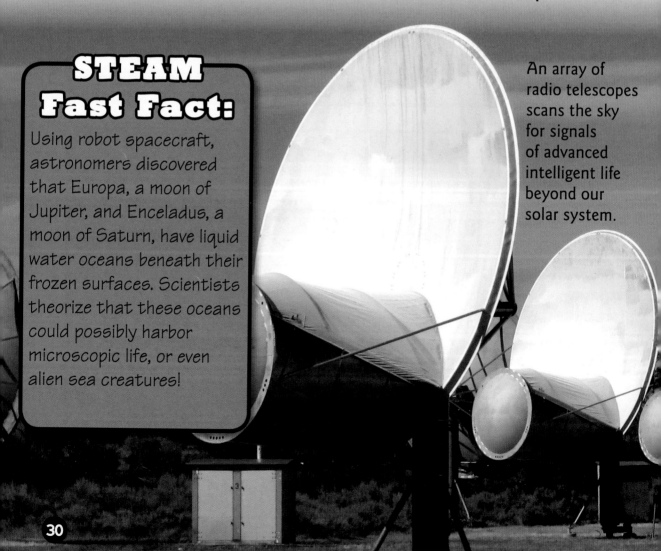

STEAM Fast Fact:

Using robot spacecraft, astronomers discovered that Europa, a moon of Jupiter, and Enceladus, a moon of Saturn, have liquid water oceans beneath their frozen surfaces. Scientists theorize that these oceans could possibly harbor microscopic life, or even alien sea creatures!

An array of radio telescopes scans the sky for signals of advanced intelligent life beyond our solar system.

Real STEAM Job: *Planetary Geologist*

Planetary geologists travel to locations on Earth that look like regions found on other planets.

When volcanoes were discovered on Jupiter's moon Io, planetary geologists went to Hawaii and Iceland to study volcano formation. When *New Horizons* sent back data for glaciers on Pluto, scientists traveled to cold regions like Antarctica. And when astronomers discovered exactly what rocks are found in comets, they studied similar rocks on Earth.

A geologist studies volcanoes on Earth to understand volcanoes on other planets and moons.

STEAM Spotlight

For a long time, astronomers theorized there were planets outside of our solar system. Scientists proved the theory in 1988, by making observations of stars. They noticed that from time to time, stars dimmed, then brightened again. Astronomers realized this occurred because planets were passing in front of those distant stars as they orbited.

Since then, more than 3,000 exoplanetary systems have been discovered. Most of the credit goes to the Kepler Space Telescope, launched in 2009 to find Earth-size planets around other stars.

Kepler discovered planets bigger than Jupiter orbiting as close to its sun as Mercury orbits our own. The space telescope also found an exoplanet that might be made entirely of diamond, and more than 500 rocky worlds that are larger than Earth and could have liquid water oceans.

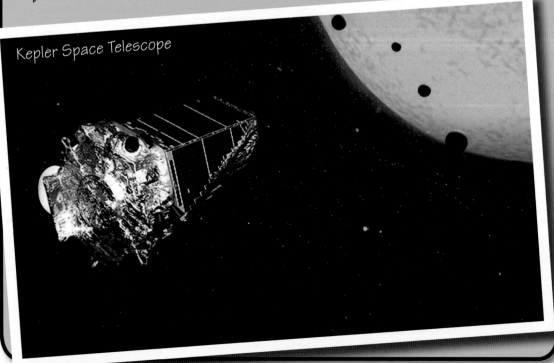
Kepler Space Telescope

STEAM in Action!

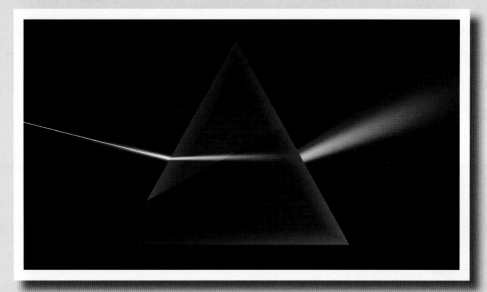

Astronomers determine the chemical compositions of stars with known exoplanets using a method called spectroscopy.

Spectroscopy breaks down visible light, like sunlight, which looks white, into a spectrum of different colors. Combined with two other methods that compare those colors to the different wavelengths that specific gasses emit, astronomers can determine the physical composition of stars.

You can see how visible light separates into different colors of the spectrum by using a prism. Hold up the prism to a light source, like an open window at daylight, or shine a flashlight through it. Make sure any light that goes through the prism shines on a white wall or a blank sheet of paper.

What colors do you see? Write them down or use colored pencils to draw what you observe. Try shining different colored lights through the prism. What colors do you see now?

Infinity...and Beyond

Astronomers collect data on things we can see. But other astronomers take that information and formulate theories on how the universe formed, how the universe could possibly end, and even if there are universes other than our own!

Using data from ground-based instruments and telescopes, astronomers were able to map the boundaries of the known universe.

STEAM Fast Fact:

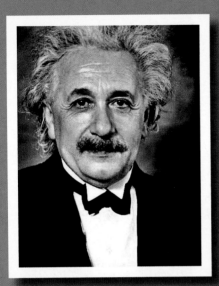

Albert Einstein
1879 – 1955

The most famous theoretical physicist is Albert Einstein. His ideas continue to influence astronomy and space exploration today. Einstein's theories on space, time, and gravity helped scientists understand the origin of the universe, called the Big Bang, and its continued expansion. Yes, even after its birth 13.7 million years ago, the universe is still growing bigger!

Real STEAM Job:
Theoretical Physicist

Theoretical physicists seek to understand the physical laws governing nature. They study forces such as light, gravity, and magnetism. Then they create mathematical equations based on these forces to illustrate how the universe works.

Theoretical physicists focus solely on research. Some are college professors. Others work for NASA's space programs or private aerospace companies to help them refine products and services.

STEAM in Action!

Gravity is one of the most powerful forces in nature. It keeps us from spinning into space. Gravity also keeps the Earth in orbit around the sun. You can feel it when you jump up—you come back down because of gravity.

To find out more about how gravity works, gather three paperclips, string, a stick, tape, a metal ruler or strip, three strong magnets, and some blocks to stack.

Tie a piece of string to each paperclip, then tape the open end of each string to the stick. Make sure you tape them evenly across the length of the stick. Now lift the stick and watch what the dangling paperclips do. Where do they point? Tilt the stick to the right or left. What happened? You are observing the force of gravity!

Cosmologists study the vast expanse of the universe. This map, from left to right, shows increasing distances and scale, starting from Earth and ending at the limit of the known universe, shows our planet is nothing more than a faint dot in the entire observable universe.

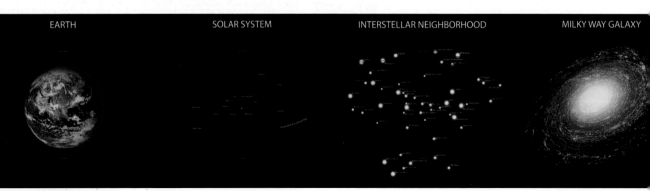

EARTH   SOLAR SYSTEM   INTERSTELLAR NEIGHBORHOOD   MILKY WAY GALAXY

Now take the magnets and put them on the metal ruler, spaced evenly like the paperclips on the string.

Place the ruler with the magnets facing down, with each end of the ruler resting on a block. Take the stick with the paperclips and put it under the magnets, making sure each paperclip is lined up with each magnet.

Describe what you see. In this example, the force of magnetism was stronger than gravity!

Real STEAM Job:
Cosmologist

Cosmologists use observational data and the most current theories to answer big questions: Did anything exist before The Big Bang? Exactly how big is our universe? When will our universe end and how?

Cosmology looks at the big picture and is basically the "study of the large-scale properties of the universe as a whole," according to NASA.

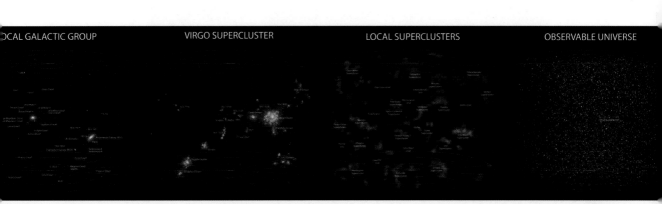

LOCAL GALACTIC GROUP   VIRGO SUPERCLUSTER   LOCAL SUPERCLUSTERS   OBSERVABLE UNIVERSE

STEAM Spotlight

One of cosmology's biggest discoveries is the evidence of "dark matter."

Scientists say that the observable universe—the stars, planets, and galaxies we see with our eyes and telescopes—make up only 4 percent of the entire universe. The other 96 percent is filled with an unknown force or energy that cannot be seen, detected, or even easily understood—hence the name "dark matter."

But how do astronomers know dark matter even exists? Because scientists can observe the gravitational influence of dark matter on things that we can see, like galaxies. So the universe, which is vast to begin with, is mostly filled with invisible stuff!

Astronomers observed light from distant objects bending before it reached Earth, which is a telltale sign of the presence of dark matter.

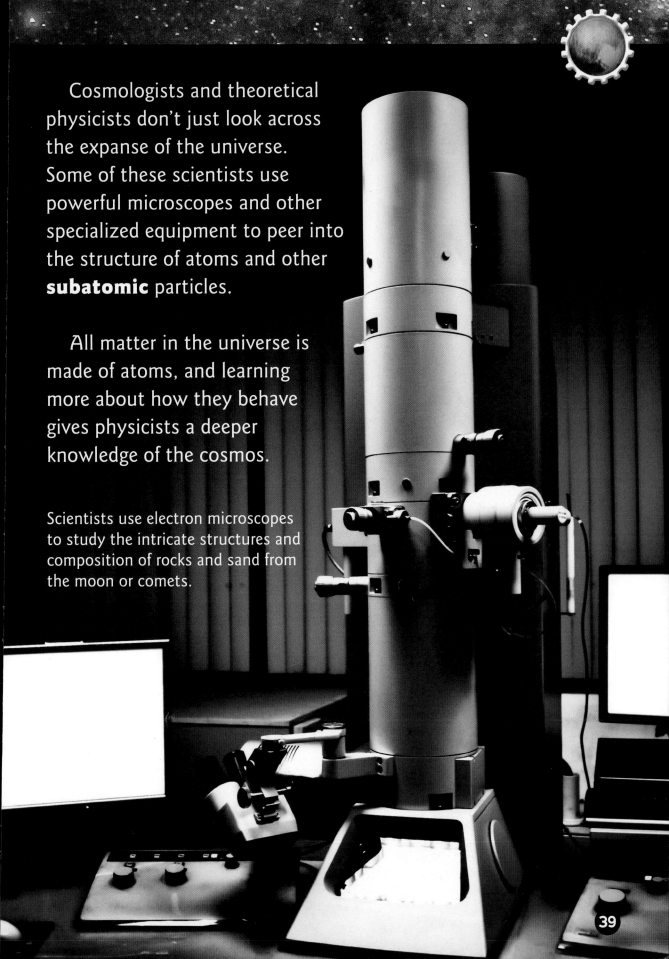

Cosmologists and theoretical physicists don't just look across the expanse of the universe. Some of these scientists use powerful microscopes and other specialized equipment to peer into the structure of atoms and other **subatomic** particles.

All matter in the universe is made of atoms, and learning more about how they behave gives physicists a deeper knowledge of the cosmos.

Scientists use electron microscopes to study the intricate structures and composition of rocks and sand from the moon or comets.

STEAM Fast Fact:

The Large Hadron Collider (LHC) in Switzerland is the largest machine in the world. Scientists run experiments by sending particles around its 17-mile (27.36 kilometer) circumference, smashing atoms together to generate even smaller subatomic units.

The LHC was built to help physicists prove theories about dark matter, the creation of the universe, and other unsolved mysteries. Scientists continue to pursue those answers!

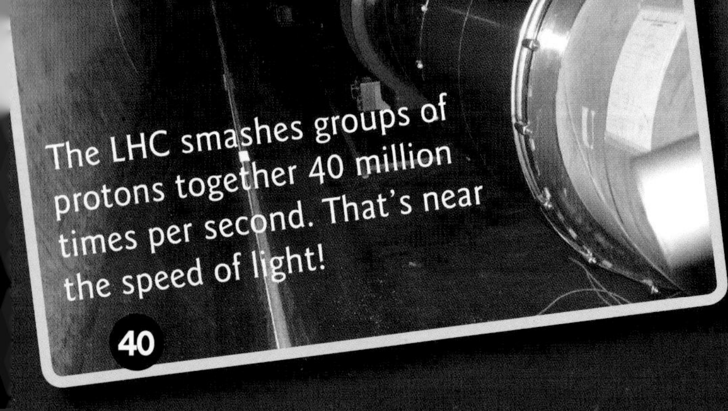

The LHC smashes groups of protons together 40 million times per second. That's near the speed of light!

Computer Programming for the Space Age

Space Age space explorers use special tools to do their jobs: telescopes to view the heavens, robots to explore planets, and rockets to voyage to space. All these machines need computer engineers to build software and run programs to collect important data or reach their far-flung destinations.

STEAM in Action!

The calculators you can find at school or in your home are more powerful than the computers used by NASA to put astronauts on the moon!

The computers of the Apollo mission had 64K of memory and the processors ran at 0.043Mhz.

Go to your computer and find out its technical specifications. How fast is your computer compared to the computers from the 1960s?

Do you have a game console like a Playstation or an Xbox? How fast does it run compared to the Apollo mission computers?

Modern pocket calculators have far more memory and processing power than the computers used in the Apollo 9 mission.

With future missions planned for the moon, Mars, and beyond, STEAM workers in space exploration will advance our knowledge of the universe and have opportunities to explore other worlds. In space exploration, the sky is not the limit!

Real STEAM Job: *Computer engineer*

More than 60 percent of the functions at NASA require engineers. The space agency looks for computer engineers and computer scientists to program code and create software that guide spacecraft to distant planets, instruct spacesuits to monitor vital signs, and tell deep space probes where to point cameras to send photos back to Earth.

STEAM Job Facts

Spacesuit Engineer

Important Skills: attention to detail, logistic problem solving, ability to work in engineering teams

Important Knowledge: structural principles, mathematics, electronics

College Major: mechanical engineering, materials science

Avionics Engineer

Important Skills: complex problem-solving, systems analysis, judgement and decision making

Important Knowledge: computer science, electronics, aerodynamics

College Major: mechanical, electrical or computer engineering

Materials Engineer

Important Skills: diagnosing problems, technical communication, optimizing solutions

Important Knowledge: energy storage, product design process, mechanics

College Major: applied physics or chemistry

Observational Astronomer

Important Skills: attention to detail, analytical thinking, careful observation

Important Knowledge: computers, natural science, mathematics

College Major: astronomy or physics

Planetary Geologist

Important Skills: critical thinking, innovation, visualization

Important Knowledge: physical science, natural science, history

College major: geology, astronomy

Computer Engineer

Important Skills: logical thinking, data interpretation, math

Important Knowledge: coding languages, mathematical modeling, complex problem-solving

College major: computer science, math

Glossary

aerospace (AIR-oh-speys): the industry concerned with the design and manufacturing of aircraft or rockets

avionics (ey-vee-ON-iks): the science and technology of development and use of electrical devices in aircraft or spacecraft

composite (kuhm-POZ-it): material made of two or more separate parts or ingredients

extrasolar (ek-struh-SOH-ler): outside of the solar system

extraterrestrial (ek-struh-tuh-RES-tree-uhl): outside, or originating outside, the limits of Earth

pressurized (PRESH-uh-rized): maintained at a level comfortable for breathing

prototype (PROH-tuh-tipe): the original model on which something is based

radiation (rey-dee-AY-shun): the process in which energy is emitted in particles or waves

subatomic (sub-uh-TOM-ik): of or relating to the processes inside an atom

vacuum (VAK-yoom): a space without matter or air

Index

Show What You Know

1. What does STEAM stand for?
2. What STEAM job requires knowledge of protecting spacecraft from the heat of reentering Earth's atmosphere?
3. What is cosmology?
4. Who was the first astronaut in space?
5. What space telescope was used to find extrasolar planets?

Websites to Visit

www.nasa.gov

www.space.com

www.astronomy.com

About the Author

Ray Reyes is a freelance photographer, former newspaper reporter, and backyard astronomer. He frequently goes out in the middle of the night to photograph stars and the Milky Way. In his free time he enjoys reading, spending time with family and friends, traveling, and binge-watching television shows.

Meet The Author!
www.meetREMauthors.com

www.rourkeeducationalmedia.com

PHOTO CREDITS: Cover images form Shutterstock.com: Milky Way© Apisit Kontong, Astronaut2© Vadim Sadovski, observatory© Tyler Rooke, Mars rover© Triff; cover images from NASA: New Horizons Spacecraft and ISS; pages 4-5 © NASA, Allexxandar; pages 6-7 © NASA, Yuri Gagarin © Zvonimir Atletic; page 8 © Philip Lange (JSC), pages 9, 10, 11, 12, 13, 14, 15 © NASA, page 16 © NASA/Chris Gunn, NASA Langley/Sean Smith, page 17 © Nadezda Murmakova; page 18 © NASA, page 19 © Pajoy sirikhanth; page 20/21 © NASA/Dimitri Gerondidakis; page 22-23 © Regent Satriandhana, page 22 telescope © John A Davis, page 23 © NASA; page 24-25 © Blue Ice, page 25 © Vector FX; page 26 New Horizons © NASA, Pluto © NASA-JHUAPL-SWRI; page 27, 28 © NASA, photos from Hubble © Image credit: ESA/Hubble & NASA, page 29 © Allexxandar; page 30-31 © Paulo Afonso, page 31 © USGS; page 32 © NASA, page 33 © Anita Ponne; page 34 © NASA, page 35 © ImageFlow; page 36-37 © Andrew Z. Colvin https://creativecommons.org/licenses/by-sa/3.0/deed.en ; page 38 © NASA; page 39 © Pan Xunbin; page 40-41, 41, 42, 43 © NASA, page 40 The Large Hadron Collider © alpinethread https://creativecommons.org/licenses/by-sa/2.0/ ,

Edited by: Keli Sipperley

Cover and Interior design by: Nicola Stratford   www.nicolastratford.com

Library of Congress PCN Data

STEAM Jobs in Space Exploration / Ray Reyes
(STEAM Jobs You'll Love)
  ISBN 978-1-68342-397-3 (hard cover)
  ISBN 978-1-68342-467-3 (soft cover)
  ISBN 978-1-68342-563-2 (e-Book)
Library of Congress Control Number: 2017931288

Rourke Educational Media
Printed in the United States of America, North Mankato, Minnesota